T0130524

Not a Millionaire, but a Kingdomaire

Delton Fernander

ISBN: 978-1-4269-4809-1 (sc)
ISBN: 978-1-4269-4974-6 (e)

Trafford rev. 11/19/2010

 www.trafford.com

North America & international
toll-free: 1 888 232 4444 (USA & Canada)
phone: 250 383 6864 ♦ fax: 812 355 4082

DEDICATION

This book is lovingly dedicated to my partner in life. The woman of my dreams and my best friend, my wife Lady Calpurnia Fernander, thank you for loving and supporting me.

When God gave you to me, I received His very best. Only God can love you more than I do. God's best in our lives is yet to come!

To Caleb Delton and Delyn Celeste our miracle gifts from God, every time I look at both of you I am amazed and reminded of the love and miraculous works God performs for his children. Both of you are destined for greatness.

PREFACE

God has given us His word, a clear set of practical instructions on how to live a fulfilled life. The scripture teaches us about the real issues of life, about love, sex, marriage, career and our goals in life. The word is a lamp unto our feet. It lights our way to success in life. The idea that God wants us successful in every area of our life may be too radical for some to handle, but that is the naked truth of God's word.

To understand God's success plan for our life we have to go back to the book of beginnings. In Genesis 1:28, the Bible says:

[28]And God blessed them, and God said unto them, Be fruitful, and multiply, and replenish the earth, and subdue it: and have dominion over the fish of the sea, and over the fowl of the air, and over every living thing that moveth upon the earth.

Created to have dominion was God's original idea. Man was never to be subjected to the torment of poverty, pain, diseases or any other similar problems.

Success in life is never a matter of chance, social background or level of educational attainment. Yes these attributes with God can play a role in one's ability to prosper in life. However the key factor to a continuous life cycle of abundance has to do with the power of your choice.. You cannot succeed unless you choose and are determined to. Your decision and overwhelming commitment to pursue your dreams and goals sets you on the path to abundant living and success.

Financial success means winning in the area of finance. Success means freedom from fears, frustrations and failure. Freedom to be all you were created to and can be. God did not create anyone to crawl through life in frustration and regrets. Mediocre living was never God's plan for man. No one can hold you down but you. Decide to move ahead in life. Decide to reach your maximum potential. Decide to reach the top of potentials. Decide to live and stay at the top.....according to the promise in Deu.28:13

[13]And the LORD shall make thee the head, and not the tail; and thou shalt be above only, and thou shalt not be beneath; if that thou hearken unto the commandments of the LORD thy God, which I command thee this day, to observe and to do them:

Believe! Really believe you can prosper financially God's way and you will. Faith is the trigger that releases God's power within you, and links you with God's unlimited resources.

INTRODUCTION

Doubt and unbelief will rob you of your strength and sap you of your courage to press on and break through life's barriers. There are self created barriers as well as satanic imposed barriers...all designed to stop you from advancing in the direction of your dream and destiny. To breakthrough these obstacles, to remove these roadblocks out of our life, there must be a complete mental 'make-over". Our thinking must change.

You must commit to thinking God's thoughts. Negativity will stifle your creative potentials and rob you of the joy of living in God's abundant provisions. Think doubt and you will fail. Think victory and you will succeed. When faced with difficult situations, instead of thinking:

I am not sure what the outcome will be...think and say I will win, the outcome is going to be favorable to me "Never think or say I can't". Instead believe God's word concerning the situation. Believe in your God-given ability to and say according to Phil.4:13 "I can do all things...through Christ"

[13]I can do all things through Christ which strengtheneth me.

Table of Contents

Chapter 1

How the enemy steals our finances

Poverty is the condition below that of ease and comfortable living and that is in all areas of life. Too many people are hungry and hurting. Too many people are poor and stranded in life's journey. Too many people are ignorant of God's abundant blessings for them and this is so tragic. A Poverty-mentality is satanic slavery! Prosperity does not create enmity with God. Abraham was a super-prosperous man, yet the Bible described him as "the Friend of God" (James 2: 23).

Prospering in what we do is part of our new identity in Christ. If you don't demonstrate it, then you are being robbed of a great part of your redemption. Supernatural supplies are a reality. The Bible is full of proofs establishing this.

Prosperity is not just having money; it's a state of well-being which you enter into through the covenant of abundance. It is deliverance from the pain and discomfort of life.

Prosperity is more than the availability of cash, it is a rich encounter of truth about the real you, your new identity in Christ and understanding God's riches within you. This understanding 'creates' wealth instead of just 'receiving wealth'.

Get set as we take an adventure into the realms of plenty. When you have a grasp of the world of prosperity, when you encounter the truth about kingdom prosperity, you just prosper. You live in a state of no-lack, a state of continuous provision.

It's time to get your life lined up with God's word. We're not in a game, this is a covenant matter. And your understanding of that covenant makes the difference.

This day will mark the breaking forth of heaven's light and favor in your life! May you experience refreshing showers of Heavens blessing in your life as you continue to read this book.

This is the hour of your prosperity and freedom! Your financial struggles must cease, now! In Jesus Name.

3 John verse 2:

²Beloved, I wish above all things that thou mayest prosper and be in health, even as thy soul prospereth.

To be prosperous means having enough, having God's provisions to enforce good on the earth, to fulfill your divine assignment and purpose in life. Satan's plan is to stop you, hinder you when it comes to you fulfilling your financial purpose in life, but in the Name of Jesus, as you soak your self in God's word, meditate on His promises the enemy will fail and you must prosper.

Financial abundance is great and very important to life here. God's will is a 'holistic' provision and abundance. There are other areas you should be enjoying God's blessing of prosperity.

Mental Prosperity - Mental prosperity is about having an abundance mentality. It is accepting the fact that there are no scarcity in this world, and that there really is enough resource and wealth in the world for every one born into this world.
A mentally prosperous person is not driven by a fear of lack or loss, so they do not act in desperation. They can enjoy the present moment and be able to give and still be generous.

Emotional Prosperity - Emotional prosperity means one is fully human, they give and receive. The joy of the Lord is their strength. They choose to be happy and share the same happiness with others around them. Emotionally healthy, they have more space in their heart to accept the shortcomings of others..

Physical Prosperity - Physical prosperity is about having good health and physical fitness. It means freedom from tormenting sickness and disease. This is one form of blessing people take for granted the most. When people are healthy, they do not appreciate just how fantastic good health is. It is one of those things that money can't always buy. And when you lack strong vibrant health, it limits you in many ways.

Poverty is a curse. It is an inability to rise and make significant progress in life. It is not from God. It's a result of either lack of knowledge or breaking God's divine principles and laws.

God's word says in Deuteronomy 28:15-17

[15]But it shall come to pass, if thou wilt not hearken unto the voice of the LORD thy God, to observe to do all his commandments and his statutes which I command thee this day; that all these curses shall come upon thee, and overtake thee:
[16]Cursed shalt thou be in the city, and cursed shalt thou be in the field.
[17]Cursed shall be thy basket and thy store.

And in vs. 38-40

[38]Thou shalt carry much seed out into the field, and shalt gather but little in; for the locust shall consume it.
[39]Thou shalt plant vineyards, and dress them, but shalt neither drink of the wine, nor gather the grapes; for the worms shall eat them.
[40]Thou shalt have olive trees throughout all thy coasts, but thou shalt not anoint thyself with the oil; for thine olive shall cast his fruit.

When Jesus died, he redeemed us from the curse of the law. The consequence of breaking His laws includes poverty, the inability to rise and stay on the top of failures. The price has been paid. The claim of justice has been satisfied by His death on Calvary's cross. The blood has been shed. Your prosperity has been paid for. Your health has been paid for.

Revelation 5:12

4

[12]Saying with a loud voice, Worthy is the Lamb that was slain to receive power, and riches, and wisdom, and strength, and honour, and glory, and blessing.

Since the price has been paid, Since He has redeemed you from the curse; you should be living in the fullness of God's provisions. You have been redeemed from pain and poverty. Do not let the devil steal your blessings any more. If you are struggling financially ...then the devil is stealing from you. Stop him, by the force of your faith. The Bible commands you to resist him and he will flee from you.

James 4:7

[7]Submit yourselves therefore to God. Resist the devil, and he will flee from you.

It is time to scare the devil off your finances, through applying God's wisdom in the area of your finance. The Bible tells us we have been called to rule in life.

Romans 5:17

[17]For if by one man's offence death reigned by one; much more they which receive abundance of grace and of the gift of righteousness shall reign in life by one, Jesus Christ.

The reason that people's financ e is being stolen from them today is because of ignorance perpetuated by Satan fighting preachers who talk about money. He does everything to stop the truth of God's word in the area of our finances. He knows the more ignorance, the more he strips believers of their God-given right to prosper. Let's not be ignorant of how he steals.

Chapter 2

God wants you to Prosper

" **¹Praise ye the LORD. Blessed is the man that feareth the LORD, that delighteth greatly in his commandments.**

²His seed shall be mighty upon earth: the generation of the upright shall be blessed.

³Wealth and riches shall be in his house: and his righteousness endureth for ever. "(Psalm 112:1-3)

Most of us have not been taught biblical prosperity. Instead, we have been taught that God wants to "humble his people by keeping them poor." But that is far from what the Bible teaches God provided the first humans with everything they needed in the Garden of Eden. However, when they listened to the voice of the serpent and doubted God's Word, they came under Satan's rule. Mankind became cursed.

God's Word clearly says prosperity is a blessing from God... in Deuteronomy 29:5,9, 30:5-9,.

[5]And I have led you forty years in the wilderness: your clothes are not waxen **old upon you, and thy shoe is not waxen old upon thy foot.**

[9]**Keep therefore the words of this covenant, and do them, that ye may prosper in all that ye do.**

Chapter 30:5-9

[5]**And the LORD thy God will bring thee into the land which thy fathers possessed, and thou shalt possess it; and he will do thee good, and multiply thee above thy fathers.**

[6]**And the LORD thy God will circumcise thine heart, and the heart of thy seed, to love the LORD thy God with all thine heart, and with all thy soul, that thou mayest live.**

[7]**And the LORD thy God will put all these curses upon thine enemies, and on them that hate thee, which persecuted thee.**

[8]**And thou shalt return and obey the voice of the LORD, and do all his commandments which I command thee this day.**

[9]And the LORD thy God will make thee plenteous in every work of thine hand, in the fruit of thy body, and in the fruit of thy cattle, and in the fruit of thy land, for **good: for the LORD will again rejoice over thee for good, as he rejoiced over thy fathers**:

God's original plan of ABUNDANCE for mankind has never changed. The God of Paradise later made a covenant of prosperity with the human race through Abraham. And Abraham became extremely rich in Genesis 17:1-9.

Abraham's descendants Isaac, Jacob and Joseph all became very wealthy according to Genesis 26:13-14. 30:43, 33:11, 39:2-3.

God's covenant worked under even the most adverse circumstances. Joseph prospered even when thrown into prison. And when the Egyptians enslaved all the Hebrews, God delivered them out of bondage (Exodus 2:24).

God's covenant men were the wealthiest men of their day. They became exceedingly wealthy, lived to a ripe old age, and died satisfied. Everything they did prospered, because God instructed them through Moses to keep the words of his covenant.

God's blessings for Abraham and his descendants were comprehensive...

"The Lord will command the blessing on you in your barns, and in all that you put your hand to...the Lord will make you abundantly prosperous, in the fruit of your body, and in the fruit of your cattle, and in the fruit of your ground..."" (Deut 28:8,11)

The promises continue...

"The Lord will open to you his good treasure in the sky, to give the rain of your land in its season, and to bless

8

all the work of your hand: and you shall lend to many nations, and you shall not borrow." (Deut 28:12)

And then God sums up his will for his people...

"Keep therefore the words of this covenant, and do them, that you may prosper in all that you do." (Deut. 29:9)

Yes God's covenant of prosperity for his people was comprehensive. But..The old covenant was also incomplete... because it couldn't change your heart (Galatians 3:21).

Christ's New Covenant

So through the centuries, God planned and worked to bring Jesus Christ into the earth. Christ fulfilled God's covenant with Abraham and established a new, better covenant.

[32]And we declare unto you glad tidings, how that the promise which was made unto the fathers,

[33]God hath fulfilled the same unto us their children, in that he hath raised up Jesus again; as it is also written in the **second psalm, Thou art my Son, this day have I begotten thee.**

[6]**But now hath he obtained a more excellent ministry, by how much also he is the mediator of a better covenant, which was established upon better promises.**(Acts 13:32-33; Hebrew 8:6).

As God's child you are Abraham's heir and God will bless you just as He blessed Abraham. He will establish his covenant with you in your generation. And prosperity is part of the covenant.

God paints a picture of your future prosperity and abundance by describing your heavenly home as a place of gold, precious stones and pearls (Revelation 21:18-21). God himself loves nice things and has nice things in store for you.

God takes great pleasure in prospering you, right now..."**He who trusts in the Lord will prosper**" (Proverbs 28:25)

"Remember the Lord your God, for it is he who gives you power to get wealth; that he may establish his covenant which he swore to your fathers, as at this day." (Deut. 8:18).

"And God is able to make all grace abound to you, that you, always having all sufficiency in everything, may abound to every good work...you will be made rich in every way so that you can always be generous." (2 Corinthians 9:8, 11).

You are an heir of God. And God will go to any length to establish his covenant with you. He even sent his own son (Romans 8:32).You have all the blessings of the old covenant plus the sonship and power of the new! God has now placed Satan under your feet and given you authority to defeat him on earth.

To share in Abraham's blessings, you must share also in his faith. Abraham was blessed because he believed what God said.

You have A God-given Right To Prosper

You have a right to prosper. Two thousand years ago Jesus Christ hung on the cross to free you from the "curse of the law" (Galatians 3:13). And a big part of that curse was poverty.

Read that curse for yourself. Paul is quoting from the book of Deuteronomy there in his letter to the Galatians. And you need to read that passage for yourself, especially chapters 27-30.

God speaks through Moses, warning his people of the terrible curses that will surely come upon them when they don't walk with him. God also tells them they will be blessed if they choose to walk with him and obey him. God does not want you cursed with poverty. He wants you to prosper.

In fact you have the same divine right to prosperity as you do for health. It's all in the covenant! It was all provided for you 2,000 years ago by Jesus Christ on the cross. You should refuse lack just as you refuse sickness.

Jesus paid a heavy price for prosperity. On the cross Jesus bore the curse of poverty just as he bore the curse of sickness and disease (Deuteronomy 28; Galatians 3:13). You should deeply appreciate all his benefits and refuse to live in lack. Believe God to fulfill his entire covenant in your life.

God wants you to enjoy peace in your life and you cannot be peaceful if your needs are not met. Peace and prosperity go together.

Chapter 3

God's Angels and your Prosperity

God's angels do his will. And God's good pleasure is the prosperity of his servants (Psalm 35:27). All the way through the Bible we see God's angels ministering Abraham's covenant to his people. Angels even gave man the Law (Galatians 3:19).

God has countless multitudes of angels constantly working on your behalf, behind the scenes.

[14]Are they not all ministering spirits, sent forth to minister for them who shall be heirs of salvation?

[22]But ye are come unto mount Sion, and unto the city of the living God, the heavenly Jerusalem, and to an innumerable company of angels,

[17]And Elisha prayed, and said, LORD, I pray thee, open his eyes, that he may see. And the LORD opened the eyes of the young man; and he saw: and, behold, the

mountain was full of horses and chariots of fire round about Elisha.(Hebrews 1:14, 12:22; 2 Kings 6:17).

Those angels will bring to pass whatever you say that is in line with God's Word (Daniel 10:12). Confess God's Word and put your angels to work.

They will prosper you just like employees prosper a corporation. Even more so...God's angels operate in the supernatural realm!

God's power is unlimited and so is his great desire to bless us. He will even go beyond his covenant promises—beyond all you can ask or think! (Ephesians 3:20). Remember, God made Abraham extremely rich and blessed him in all things (Genesis 24:34-35).

Don't stagger at God's promises through unbelief. Be like Abraham and become fully persuaded that God can do what he's promised (Romans 4:20-21).

Receiving Kingdom Prosperity

Put God first in your life. Jesus says seek first God's kingdom and his righteousness and God will provide you with everything you need in life (Mat. 6:33). God wants you to have plenty so you can stay out of debt and have an abundance left over to help others.

Trust in God, not your possessions

Jesus said beware of covetousness. Set your affections on things above, and God will bless you with prosperity.

Your source of prosperity is God's Word, not people. Look only to God.

Meditate on God's Word

Time spent meditating on God's Word will erase all doubts from your heart. Until you believe that Word more than Satan, circumstances, or people. Meditate on the prosperity scriptures until they become reality. Then act upon them. The Word grows by believing it, speaking it, and acting upon it.

Walk by faith, not by sight

Believe what God says regardless of what you feel or see with your eyes. Make your thoughts, actions, and words agree with what God says. Train your senses to react with God's Word. Get to the place where you never waiver.

Study the Word for yourself

Use CDs, meetings, newsletters, books, whatever, to get God's Word into your heart. When you are filled with God's Word, it is hard for Satan to even get your attention.

Speak God's Word that covers your need

Jesus said you are to speak to the mountain, speak to the obstacle in your life (Mark 11:23-24). You not only can have what you say, you do have what you say. So believe that every word you speak comes to pass.

God's Word is law in the spiritual realm. Think about that. You are the voice of God in the earth. Your voice carries authority in both worlds.

Do not tolerate any lack in your life. You are entitled to all of Abraham's blessings. Prosperity belongs to you and the angels know how to help you prosper!

Satan tells you "there is no way," but Jesus says, "I am the way". As God's son or daughter you have the same authority over the earth that Adam had in the Garden of Eden. And as you speak God's Word you put the angels to work (Hebrews 1:14).

Stand on God's Word! Put on God's armor and stand your ground. Determine to stand forever if necessary and receive your covenant prosperity. God is not pleased if you draw back in fear (Hebrews10:35-39).

When Satan says God's Word is not working, recognize that as a lie. Satan still tries to discredit God's Word, just as he did with Eve. The only thing he has to use against you is lies and deception.

Keep confessing God's prosperity promises. Cast down all of your imaginations and thoughts that exalt themselves against God's Word. Never give place to the devil, but resist him (2 Corinthians 10:5, Ephesians 4:27, James 4:7).

Be like Shadrach, Meshach, and Abednego who would not bow down to pressure—and they did not burn. They walked out of that burning furnace without even the smell of smoke on them. God sent his angel to enforce his covenant for these men! (Daniel 3)

You, too, must determine to come out of your financial trials without even the smell of defeat! Resist the devil with the words of your mouth. This forces him to flee. Satan knows that you have whatever you say. So he is after your words. Don't let the world's "evil pirate" plunder your goods.

There is a principle of sowing and reaping. When you sow your life into God's hands, you reap eternal life and heaven. These laws operate and function in all areas of life. If you plant corn you will not harvest peas. Whatever you sow is what you reap. What ever seed you plant you will reap in kind. If you sow hate and meanness you will receive the same. The word says we reap what we sow:.Gal.6:7,8

[7]Be not deceived; God is not mocked: for whatsoever a man soweth, that shall he also reap.
[9]And let us not be weary in well doing: for in due season we shall reap, if we faint not.

On the other hand if you sow love, kindness and friendliness you will reap abundance of the same. Some people say "people don't care about me" The question is, do you care about people? Do you love unconditionally? Do you lavishly give of your love to those who do not deserve your love? The truth is you reap what you sow….and not less..

Most Christians do not look for or expect to receive anything in return for their giving. So they get nothing for they expected nothing and believed for nothing.

Another reason for lack and insufficiency is disobedience. Receiving has a blessing, but giving has a far greater blessing. God has no favorite in His Kingdom.

16

He wants you blessed as much as every one else. He wants all prosperous and successful and that again includes you. He desires all of His children to enjoy the abundant living that comes through giving.

You say, "I believe God wants me to prosper, I am too blessed to be stressed, I am the head and not the tail," you may confess and claim your prosperity all day. If you don't do MORE than just confess, nothing! I mean absolutely nothing changes for you!

James 2:17-26

[17]Even so faith, if it hath not works, is dead, being alone.
[18]Yea, a man may say, Thou hast faith, and I have works: shew me thy faith without thy works, and I will shew thee my faith by my works.
[19]Thou believest that there is one God; thou doest well: the devils also believe and tremble.
20But wilt thou know, O vain man, that faith without works is dead?
[21]Was not Abraham our father justified by works, when he had offered Isaac his son upon the altar?
22Seest thou how faith wrought with his works, and by works was faith made perfect?
[23]And the scripture was fulfilled which saith, Abraham believed God, and it was imputed unto him for righteousness: and he was called the Friend of God.
[24]Ye see then how that by works a man is justified, and not by faith only.
[25]Likewise also was not Rahab the harlot justified by works, when she had received the messengers, and had sent them out another way?
[26]For as the body without the spirit is dead, so faith without works is dead also.

Do you want this abundance promised in God's word? Then you must put action to your faith. The action and the life-style of giving ushers you to a continuous cycle of receiving and abundance. Luke 6:38

38Give, and it shall be given unto you; good measure, pressed down, and shaken together, and running over, shall men give into your bosom. For with the same measure that ye mete withal it shall be measured to you again.

Do you want to receive? Then give first. Every farmer understands this principle. He sows his seeds and patiently waits for the harvest .Gal.6:9

9And let us not be weary in well doing: for in due season we shall reap, if we faint not.

Your harvest is guaranteed. Your reward of faithful sowing will surely come. When the seed leaves your hand, it goes into your future as a harvest. Don't give up "in well doing". God does not go back on his promises.11 Corinthians 9:10

10Now he that ministereth seed to the sower both minister bread for your food, and multiply your seed sown, and increase the fruits of your righteousness;

Paul in the scripture above shows us what happens when we give. You will receive as harvest all that you will need for your life. You will get more seed to sow. If you have been giving twenty dollars, you will find that you can move to fifty and then to one hundred. That is the increase of seed to sow back into God's harvest field. And your harvest will increase. In 2 Corinthians Paul wrote of the Macedonian

Churches, he tells of how the Spirit of God moved on them to give generously. 2 Corinthians 8:1-5

¹Moreover, brethren, we make known to you the grace of God bestowed on the churches of Macedonia;
²How that in a great trial of affliction the abundance of their joy and their deep poverty abounded unto the riches of their liberality.
³For to their power, I bear record, yea, and beyond their power they were willing of themselves;
⁴Praying us with much entreaty that we would receive the gift, and take upon us the fellowship of the ministering to the saints.
⁵And this they did, not as we hoped, but first gave their own selves to the Lord, and unto us by the will of God.

It is important here to know that the key to the Macedonian generosity was in the fact that .."They gave themselves first to the Lord". Do not give your money to God if you are unwilling to give Him your life. You cannot buy God's favor. He wants you first, and then out of the giving of yourself will come the grace of giving. Give yourself to God. Abide in right relationship with Him and His word. Your life will never be barren of God's blessings. 2 Corinthians 8:7

⁷Therefore, as ye abound in every thing, in faith, and utterance, and knowledge, and in all diligence, and in your love to us, see that ye abound in this grace also.

The proof of your love is revealed in your giving. Paul again admonished the Corinthian churches and believers to show proof of their love by their giving.

2 Corinthians 8:24

[24]**Wherefore shew ye to them, and before the churches, the proof of your love, and of our boasting on your behalf.**

2 Corinthians 9:9

[9]**As it is written, He hath dispersed abroad; he hath given to the poor: his righteousness remaineth for ever.**

Psalm 37:23-26

[23]**The steps of a good man are ordered by the LORD: and he delighteth in his way.**
[24]**Though he fall, he shall not be utterly cast down: for the LORD upholdeth him with his hand.**
[25]**I have been young, and now am old; yet have I not seen the righteous forsaken, nor his seed begging bread.**
[26]**He is ever merciful, and lendeth; and his seed is blessed.**

When you are giving God's way, you can be assured that you shall not be forsaken and your seed shall not beg for bread. That's God promise.

2 Corinthians 9:8

[8]And God is able to make all grace abound toward you; that ye, always having all sufficiency in all things, may abound to every good work:

God is a seed provider. He will make the seed and money to give available.

2 Corinthians 9:10

[10]Now he that ministereth seed to the sower both minister bread for your food, and multiply your seed sown, and increase the fruits of your righteousness;

Never eat the seed you are to sow. God is and has always been the greatest giver. It is His nature to give.

John 3:16 [16]For God so loved the world that he gave his only begotten Son, that whosoever believeth in him should not perish, but have everlasting life.

Romans 8:32

[32]He that spared not his own Son, but delivered him up for us all, how shall he not with him also freely give us all things?

Ephesians 2:8,9

[8]For by grace are ye saved through faith; and that not of yourselves: it is the gift of God:
[9]Not of works, lest any man should boast.

The whole truth about financial rewards is that any giver prospers. "A generous man will prosper; he who refreshes others will himself be refreshed," (Proverbs 11:25). It does not matter whether one gives to the work of God or to the work of men. Neither does his religion or spiritual state matter. The law of seed time and harvest time applies to all of us. One harvests whatever he sows.

A mango seed will always harvest mangoes no matter the soil it is planted in. It cannot change to oranges. It is the same with material or financial seeds, that is why many people in the occult are very wealthy. They are not wealthy because they are in occultism. It is because they know and aggressively apply the law of seed time and harvest time. But they have their major problems that amount to severe bondage.

Some of what individuals and companies call charitable giving to non-profit sports clubs, schools, hospitals and communities are activities of increasing their wealth so that they can increase their mischief. Their seed is of the flesh and the material harvest is of the flesh. Whatever the sacrifice it has no reward in heaven.

He gave us His best and the most precious gift, the gift of His only begotten son. So if He did not spare His own son, nothing is too great or too good to give His children. Every one born of God has His nature. God is a giver by nature and that's our nature too. The enemy uses experiences of life, background and environment to condition people is mind against this giving nature. Selfishness and greed is never God's nature and should not be yours. Begin to see yourself as a giver. Give cheerfully and abundantly if you want to reap an abundant harvest!

2 Corinthians 9:6,7

[6]But this I say, He which soweth sparingly shall reap also sparingly; and he which soweth bountifully shall reap also bountifully.
[7]Every man according as he purposeth in his heart, so let him give; not grudgingly, or of necessity: for God loveth a cheerful giver.

Chapter 4

Obedience is the Key

Like in the old covenant era God brings whatever results based on our financial obedience or disobedience. He said to those who desired financial deliverance and freedom:

"Bring the whole tithe into the storehouse, that there may be food in my house. Test me in this and see if I will not throw open the floodgates of heaven and pour out so much blessing that you will not have room enough for it. I will prevent pests from devouring your crops and the vines in your fields will not cast their fruits, says the Lord Almighty," (Malachi 3:10-11).

So this is God's way of providing material necessities. It is through giving. A tithe (ten percent) of one's income was the minimum in the Old Testament. Something is a gift when the giver requires nothing in return. It maybe financial, material, service of one's talents and time, counsel and so on. It's something that will contribute to the well-being of someone or group at the expense of the giver's input.

Through the gifts, God says he is moved to "throw open the floodgates of heaven" to bless the giver. It may not be instant or come in a way the giver may assume. However God works everything out in his way and timing to bless the giver.

Not only does He open doors for his blessings he also prevents the enemy from undoing our blessings. You probably know people who received much only to lose it all in mysterious ways, to suffer crippling health problems or other misfortune. God works to prevent such experiences for as long as we continue obeying his word. On the highest level we're requested to:

"Seek first his kingdom and his righteousness and all these things will be given to you as well," (Matthew 6:33).

It means putting his ways of righteous living, evangelism interests and charitable interests ahead of our personal earthly interests. They need to matter to us more than our interests and needs. All the things we need for our earthly living are given to us as we pursue his interests.

God's Ways or Ours?

God has given his ways to open the floodgates of heaven. But some may decide to look for their own ways they consider more convenient. All sorts of "justifiable" excuses may come up. The most common are, "I don't have enough to give anyone," "I have so many critical obligations that giving would not be practical," "I've not yet started earning my own income." Thus we devise other ways to receive from God. We hold long prayers, sometimes accompanied with fasting. Some who misunderstand spiritual warfare resort to binding and rebuking demons from holding their material blessings.

24

At the end of the day, nothing moves. We may even begin to question ourselves: "Maybe God wants us to remain in lack?" After all, the Bible strongly warns against the love of money. So living day to day on subsistence provisions by the grace of God could be his will for our lives. All this is not true. We are only applying the wrong principles for the wrong purposes. We still end up walking in financial disobedience and harvesting fruits of financial disobedience.

Our Lord waits for us to apply what he has prescribed for us. Until we respond according to his word he continues to wait. Resorting to sinful ways and other worldly ways may work but only to bring in other worse problems in the long-run. On another note, a believer may have other issues outside giving that may be contributing to financial woes. All these are hindrances to what God has promised through his word.

Still under Manna or in Canaan?

God fed the Israelites manna during their 40 years in the wilderness. Manna was enough for the day and no more for the next. Any attempt to lay aside some for a succeeding day failed, except the day immediately preceding the Sabbath. Attempts of preservation only led to the manna to rot.

After 40 years, the disobedient generation of military age had all gone except Joshua and Caleb who had obeyed God. Then God asked Joshua to circumcise the sons of the disobedient generation. After he obeyed this and observed the Passover, God opened the door for them to eat their own produce in Canaan. The manna stopped (Joshua 5) and the Israelites were no longer bound to daily rations.

Their reproach, which was a sign of bondage, was rolled away when the new generation matured and it fulfilled its obedience through Joshua. "Today I have rolled away the reproach of Egypt from you," Joshua 5:9. Their reproach was not rolled away when they crossed the sea with Moses. It was after more than 40 years when they qualified to inherit their promised blessing. All along they were still in some form of bondage like in Egypt. It was a material bondage. No wonder they complained so much that some even asked to return to Egypt where they had no freedom.

This could be the case for some believers in their material lives. Spiritually they are no longer in bondage. Materially things have not changed or have worsened. Some even consider returning to sinful ways of gaining material means. They consider sacrificing their spiritual freedom for material gain. They have prayed and begged God for years but little if anything has changed.

Yet God is saying some are in a financial wilderness of their own making because of disobedience to his financial principles. Prayer and begging is not a requirement in this area of our Christian lives. According to his word there is a better way out than resorting to sinful or spiritually compromising ways. His ways may take longer than the sinful ways but are more than worthwhile in the long run.

So some may be living in a financial wilderness of their own making, because of their disobedience. There are only two wildernesses in life – one is God-made while the other is man-made. Jesus entered a God-made wilderness when he was led to be tempted by the devil. His wilderness was a general trial of faith and not a financial one. Our God-made financial wilderness is mostly during the years of our upbringing. We receive manna we never worked for.

26

The manna is just enough to get by and scarce enough to continue looking forward to our own means.

During this period, God wants us among other things to learn obedience and submission to higher authority. It is also training ground for our submission to God and his ways. During God's ordained wilderness our parents and guardians not only have heaven's commission to care for us, they also have the means to exercise their authority.

No wilderness is exciting. As we grow older we desire more to be free from the financial wilderness of being on the receiving end. For some, the mere thought of others sacrificing their lives for them is tormenting. They look forward to freeing their parents or guardians from their burden of looking after them. For others the manna itself becomes increasingly unbearable. And so on. A God-made financial wilderness is at least one we are not to regret. We found ourselves under particular parents or guardians of certain means and other characteristics. It was God's own design. It's a self-made one that is a problem.

Chapter 5

Financial Wilderness - A Father's Discipline

The wilderness that we can somehow live to regret for having gone through is the self-made one. It comes as a result of disobedience to God. Here an individual has the power of choice but misuses it by ignoring God's principles. In the God-made one there is nothing we can do except endure it. In the self-made one there is everything we can do to get out of it. Its presence is a sign that there is something God requires of us that we're not fulfilling.

When the Israelites disobeyed God they paid the penalty by being caged in a wilderness for forty years. They received manna just to keep them alive while paying for their sins. The same happens to us when we disobey his principles. He leaves us to survive on manna that is just enough to get by and scarce enough to continue looking forward to being free from such mere survival.

It may seem like God is a strict disciplinarian waiting to punish every disobedience. However scripture and history show that his hand of mercy is more prevalent than his hand of justice. His greatest act of mercy was having his Son, Jesus, die for our sins. We would be paying for every sin if it wasn't for Christ. For most of us who have not been perfect this would be serious bondage, worse than slavery.

So God disciplines us when we disobey his biblical financial principles. His discipline is what enables us to return to his ways when we stray. He allows a financial curse or wilderness to develop in our lives. To him disobedience to his biblical financial principles is robbery. We rob God of what belongs to him. He said, "Will a man rob God? Yet you rob me...in tithes and offerings. You are under a curse – the whole nation of you because you are robbing me" (Malachi 8-9).

A whole nation or household can be under a curse because of one of the heads of a household is walking in disobedience. The curse of not giving is living in scarcity and continual harassment from the devourer (devil) either through a financial misfortune, losses, theft, money going to cover sickness, and other unnecessary burdens. And because God is merciful, he gives manna to the disobedient so that they survive by the day. Until obedience is fulfilled the manna continues.

Breaking the Curse of Poverty Through Obedience

The curse is only changed into a blessing when one starts giving. Ten percent was the Old Covenant's minimum but it can be a safe level to start on. There is no other substitute. Our monetary and material means that are given as gifts are the only worthy seeds for a material harvest. We can also freely give our time and talents that have financial value to Christian causes. This can be a way of making up for low financial contributions in the manna years of scarcity. Merely praying or fasting will do almost nothing. Prayer and fasting only water the seeds. Without the seeds no amount of water will bring anything from the ground. No seed falling to the ground, no harvest.

Usually prayer and fasting are not necessary to material harvests This is because material seeds work on God's principle: "A man reaps whatever he sows." (Galatians 6: 7). If material harvests came from prayer then only Christians would have the material means. The rest would be on manna until they got born again. Evangelism would be so easy, if it would be needed at all. Unbelievers would seek salvation once they got tired of the manna.

God has set aside prayer (and occasional fasting) for more important seeds -evangelism. He wants us to concentrate on watering (praying and fasting) over seeds of salvation and liberty among lost souls. We can pray over our evangelism efforts or those of other ministries to produce their intended harvest of souls.

In the financial or material area God personally opens the windows of heaven to bless us. This happens as we apply the principles of seed time and harvest time. We do not need to pray or ask him to open the windows of heaven.

Here he wants to be tested and not be prayed to. Can you imagine God asking his creatures to challenge, test or tempt him? He said, "Test me in this and see if I will not throw open the floodgates of heaven and pour out so much blessings that you will not have room enough for it" (Malachi 3:10). There is so much in heaven that God had to build floodgates -figuratively speaking. Floodgates are for stopping floods. God's Kingdom is flooded with blessings waiting to be poured out on obedient souls in the biblical financial principles.

God says "test me," or "try me." In paraphrasing he is saying "let's see who is going to win in the giving game between you and me. Let's see if what you give to me will be more than what I give back in return to you." It's easy to know who the winner will be.

God's victory of giving more than the giver may not come in the short-run. Any short-sighted person can have a difficult time understanding how God works. Many times the desired means also do not come the way an individual expects. For instance, he may open doors for your children into schools and professional positions that you could only dream of. This way your children become a very exciting part of your senior life. Seeing the faithfulness of God fulfilled in their lives gives you more reasons for living. Such a blessing may take 30 or more years to materialize. Yet you kept sowing throughout those decades. God is faithful – in his time and way.

Chapter 6

How God Opens the Floodgates of Heaven

The floodgates of blessings God pours out are in the form of avenues that he opens for us to receive from him and be under his protection. One avenue is through divine ideas. For instance, God told Isaac to plant crops in drought season and he "reaped a hundred fold" (Genesis 27:12). God can drop ideas into the heart of an individual on how to run or start a particular business, where to look for employment, or if it is a promotion, how they should conduct themselves for promotion.

Another avenue is God commanding favor in the hearts of other people towards an individual and their particular calling. "Let love and faithfulness never leave you...then you will win favor and a good name in the sight of God and man," (Proverbs 3:3-4). This favor or grace is the anointing of God upon an individual and his/her particular calling.

The individual may not be as educated as their associates, or as good looking, as old or young, as talented, or whatever is desired, yet the anointing upon them will make them exceptional in one way or another. The individual can be a farmer, lawyer, nurse, retailer, an evangelist, consultant, teacher, and so on. People will be attracted to her and be more willing to receive from or transact with whatever she offers than with others.

The academic world may be the most meritorious system in the world. One gets a certificate, degree or grade depending on their ability in a selected field. Merit or ability not favor or chance is the ultimate determinant. The professional world operates in a somewhat chaotic way. Merit (ability) and favor coexist with one being more prominent than the other in different fields and places.

Making it in such a chaotic world may need more than merit for some. For others ability may be all that will be required. God opens doors for mastering the ability and where necessary grants favor in securing a position, business, property, interest or whatever.

God even lays burdens in the hearts of some people to give in monetary or material form to the individual. Our Lord Jesus and his disciples lived under this favor. Jesus made Judas Iscariot, a perpetual thief, and his treasure to show how unconcerned he was for material provisions. No matter how much Judas embezzled supplies never ran out.

How God Prevents Satan from Destroying the Blessing

"I will prevent pests from devouring your crops, and the vines in your fields will not cast their fruit," (Malachi 3:11).

Pests are problems and misfortune that arise in areas of interest in our lives. The comparison scripture uses is related to farming. A farmer labors sowing seed, tenders it while eagerly expecting a great harvest as the final outcome. However pests come and ruin all his labor. He worked hard but this time it was all in vain. He worked to feed the pests, not himself or his/her family.

In our lives Satan and his agents are the pests. They work to destroy everything we endeavor in that is godly and scriptural. Destruction is their only ministry. Their ministry succeeds where we do not have God's protection. So if our financial areas have no covering our labor may be in vain.

God prevents Satan's access when we start to apply the biblical financial principles. We do not need to pray to him to rebuke the devourer. He does it on his own. Our obedience breaks the curse of poverty for as long as we remain in obedience. We do not need to be even concerned how Satan is working in his ministry of trying to frustrate our lives. Our concern should be on how we are obeying God in fulfilling our required input.

When our obedience is fulfilled to God's principles he works to rebuke or prevent the devourer affecting our lives. Knowing God's principles in every area of our lives is therefore our only refuge. The enemy feeds on our ignorance. When we know the truth in a given area, Satan can devise any plan of destruction but God's angels will prevent him from fulfilling it. No need of binding and loosing evil spirits of this and that.

Non-believers survive by the mercy of God. The devourer has easy access into their lives. The financial area is where more people are trapped in the curse of poverty than are out of it. This includes believers. Satan may be the thief that comes to steal the blessing but he is not the problem. The problem is believers themselves. We give him access to spoil the harvest if we do not live by biblical financial principles. Living outside biblical principles gives pests as much access to us as they have to unbelievers in their finances.

For instance one may save a good amount of money only to loose it through a misfortune. An illness or accident may come along and eat some of it. He/she may invest into something only to see it collapse. One way or another, money seems to be coming in and quickly going out through another door.

Another situation may be borrowing for matters one shouldn't have. The individual could still survive without them. But the tempter shows up with wonderful ideas on how one's life will be better off if they borrowed to obtain certain desires. The funds will after all be repaid at a low interest. Before long the individual is having trouble paying the interest, let alone the loaned amount. It is like being caught up in a prison of working to pay someone else. This someone is part of the pests that have entered to eat whatever one labors in.

This is how curses operate. They keep people from making any progress in life. People try hard only to fall back, or ending up worse off. A worse off situation arises where an individual gets into increasing debts. Another can be through other problems coming up to eat every form of peace of mind one desires to have in life. We see this in many so called celebrities. Many live tormenting lives, confronting one serious problem after another. They have money and earthly fame but they have no peace. Having peace only comes from the Prince of Peace (Isaiah 9:6).

Most of us who are saved have this peace. We did not buy it. It was freely given upon receiving Jesus as our Lord and Savior. We have the most expensive blessing that no wealth, power, beauty, fame or worldly pleasure can buy. Any believer that does not have it ought to search what is grieving the Holy Spirit from bringing his peace and comfort. Sometimes trials may overwhelm but only some times. Most times the Lord enables us to bear our trials of faith, knowing he is the one in control, not our circumstances, nor other people, nor Satan.

Chapter 7

Same Harvest, Different Taste of Harvested Material Fruits

The only difference between Christian and all other forms of giving is that one sows to the Spirit (of God) and the other to the flesh (sinful nature). Monetary and material gifts by a Christian with genuine motives to other believers or needy people in society are material seeds sown to the Spirit. The recipients may include one's local church, an evangelistic ministry, and a Christian charity.

On the other hand, monetary and material gifts by a non-Christian, even with right motives, sown to needy people in society are seeds sown to the flesh. One cannot buy his/her way to heaven by good works. Good works that have value in heaven are from us who already are counted as God's children. The good hearted non-believer will be blessed materially and have quite a respectable life on earth but that's about it.

You may have met or heard of good-hearted non-Christians doing all kinds of charity work. Many lead quite admirable lives that many self-righteous Christians may have much to learn from. I have met many in various areas including in charitable ministries. I pray for their salvation which is a free gift from God. "It (salvation) is the gift of God not by works, so that no one can boast," Ephesians 2:8-9.

While salvation and a plot in heaven is a free gift through Christ, the crown is not. Christians that may think works are not important have not read the Bible. They have not read how much believers had to sacrifice for the gospel and godly work. On judgment day Jesus' judgment will be based on what we have done not just for being saved by grace. "My reward is with me, and I will give to every one according to what he has done," (Revelations 22:12).

It gets more complicated where scripture adds that not all our good works will be accepted. Like those of unbelievers some of our works may be rejected. They will have no value in heaven. They will bring material rewards here on earth. But they will not be credited in heaven.

"When God gives any man wealth and possessions, and enables him to enjoy them, to accept his lot and to be happy in his work - this is a gift of God. He seldom reflects on the days of his life (with regrets), because God keeps him occupied with gladness of heart," (Ecclesiastes 5: 19-20).

"The blessing of the Lord brings wealth, and he adds no trouble to it," (Proverbs 10:22). His blessings add no trouble because they are fruits one reaps from sowing to the Spirit.

Scripture says the fruit of sowing to the Spirit (of God) is "love, joy, peace, patience, kindness, goodness, faithfulness, gentleness and self-control," (Galatians 5: 22-23).

"The Lord's curse is on the house of the wicked, but he blesses the home of the righteous" (Proverbs 3:33). The measure of material rewards is therefore not on the scale of quantity but on quality. To what extent are they either curses or blessings on the lives of those that have them? To what extent are they facilitating their walk with God? To what extent are they blocking it? David prayed to God, "Turn my heart towards your statutes and not towards selfish gain. Turn my eyes away from worthless things," (Psalm 119:36-37).

Christianity is a call to total self-denial. Whatever comes into one's hand must go back to extending God's interests not ours. For instance, if an individual is called into business ministry, the more profits God blesses him with, the more he must sow towards God's interests. He should not stick with the Old Testament ten percent rule and shift the rest on personal gains of acquiring a fleet of cars and other unnecessary personal additions. His selflessness must be expressed in his zeal in God's interests and lack of interest in himself.

Chapter 8

Success has an attitude

A Success Attitude is a mindset that allows you to accomplish dreams and set goals. You know what you want and then develop habit and attitude that create the opportunity to achieve your dream success.

"You were taught, with regard to your former way of life, to put off your old self, which is being corrupted by its deceitful desires; to be made new in the attitude of your minds; and to put on the new self, created to be like God in true righteousness and holiness." Ephesians 4:22-24

While commissioning Solomon to build the temple, David told him:

"And you, Solomon my son, obey the God of your father and serve him with a submissive attitude and a willing spirit, for the Lord examines all minds and understands every motive of one's thoughts. If you seek him, he will

let you find him, but if you abandon him, he will reject you permanently." (1 Chronicles 28:9-10)

When you have faith in God, you will do more and attempt to do more. And you will succeed! The ancient Greeks defined faith as "action out of confidence." The more confidence you have, the more action you will take. Faith in God gives you confidence.

We were born with a deficit mentality - always aware of our guilt and "need to survive," we bustle about life just "trying to make it." This is how Satan's domain operates - you must "rule your own life," and thus you must beat out the next guy for the scarce supply of survival goods. You must hold on tightly to what you have or people will take it all, leaving you empty handed. In most places of the world, this is "reality" - there is barely enough for a few. This is not God's plan for you.

We all want success in life. We want success in our home life, business life, and in our relationships with others. The most important single factor that guarantees our success in every aspect of our lives is having a positive attitude. Without a positive attitude success is not possible. Earl Nightingale call attitude "the magic word." If you desire success, you must have the attitude.

Why did Abraham leave his family in search of God? He was tired of mediocrity!! He knew he needed a change of attitude to succeed. His undying quest led to the call he got from God. (Genesis 12:1-3)

"Now the LORD had said unto Abram, Get thee out of thy country, and from thy kindred, and from thy father's house, unto a land that I will shew thee:

And I will make of thee a great nation, and I will bless thee, and make thy name great; and thou shalt be a blessing:

And I will bless them that bless thee, and curse him that curseth thee: and in thee shall all families of the earth be blessed. "

God couldn't ignore Abraham's attitude!

You will never attract positive things into your life if all of your thoughts are negative. Just as a magnet attracts anything metal our minds attract the things we think about most. Your mind will always seek to turn the things you think about most into physical reality. Ralph Waldo Emerson wrote, "A man becomes what he thinks about, most of the time."

Charles Swindoll once wrote; "the longer I live, the more I realize the impact of attitude on life. Attitude to me is more important than facts. It is more important than the past, than education, than money, than circumstances, than failures, than success, than what other people think or say or do. It is more important than appearance, gift, or skill. It will make or break a company...a church...a home.

The remarkable thing is we have a choice every day regarding the attitude we will embrace for that day. We cannot change our past...we cannot change the fact that people will act in a certain way. We cannot change the inevitable. The only thing we can do is play on the string we have, and that is our attitude. I am convinced that life is 10 percent what happens to me and 90 percent how I react to it. And so it is with you... we are in charge of our attitudes."

Every one of us has two different minds, the conscious and the subconscious. The conscious mind is our thinking, which uses logic, deduction, reason, and sound judgments to make its decisions. Your choices in life are made by the conscious mind.

Nathan said to David, "You should do whatever you have in mind for God is with you." (1 Chronicles 17: 2)

The subconscious mind lies outside your conscious mind. It has access to data, information, and ideas outside your own experience. Your subconscious mind works 24 hours a day and it is the source of all examples of pure creativity, problem solving, and goal achievement. It is the amazing part of the human mind, the part where the genius in all of us lies.

Our subconscious mind is not able to distinguish between positive and negative thoughts. So, if you ' tell yourself' something long enough your subconscious will eventually come to believe it and if you confess something repeatedly whether it is positive or negative it will become your reality which will find ways to manifest in time.

This is because your subconscious mind constantly strives to attract the material equivalent of your most dominant thoughts and imaginations. It is impossible to have a negative mindset and then attract positive things. If you're thinking about problems constantly you will find them.

The "I will never do well" "My case is beyond redemption" I am too down to rise and too poor to be made rich"

This kind of thinking are mental poisoning and killers of success. Is it possible to overcome negative and pessimistic thinking with positive thoughts? Oh yes....we all can!

It is all a matter of renewing the mind according to Romans 12:2

And be not conformed to this world: but be ye transformed by the renewing of your mind, that ye may prove what is that good, and acceptable, and perfect, will of God.

You can train yourself to think thoughts in line with God's will for your life. You can do it....every one can learn and make it a habit of thinking God's thought; develop a kingdom mindset to enjoy a lifestyle of the kingdom. The way to do this is to commit to a discipline habit of deprogramming your mind and flushing your mind of negative destructive and success retarding thoughts by renewing your mind with God's word.

You then nurture those positive thoughts until there is no room for any negative thoughts to grow. Then, make a habit of stopping a negative thought any time it appears and replace it with a positive thought. For example, replace, "I can't do it" with "I can do it" and you'll find your attitude and your life will greatly improve.

Positive thoughts will lead you to financial success and it will help you find the true riches of life for yourself and your family. So whatever it is in life that you want, you must begin today to become a "positive thinker of God's thought" Once you do this, your future success will be unlimited.

Many people miss the path to true prosperity because they are seeking it through ungodly ways and principles. God

44

has and deals with us on the basis of His principles. God's economic principles are recession proof and are unfailing. The way to true abundance — in all areas of your life — is to discover and live in God's economic principles as reveal in the pages of the Bible.

2 Chronicles 20:20

And they rose early in the morning, and went forth into the wilderness of Tekoa: and as they went forth, Jehoshaphat stood and said, Hear me, O Judah, and ye inhabitants of Jerusalem; Believe in the LORD your God, so shall ye be established; believe his prophets, so shall ye prosper.

As Apostle Paul wrote in his first epistle to Timothy:

Command those who are rich in this world's goods not to be haughty or to set their hope on riches, which are uncertain, but on God who richly provides us with all things for our enjoyment. Tell them to do good, to be rich in good deeds, to be generous givers, sharing with others. In this way they will save up a treasure for themselves as a firm foundation for the future and so lay hold of what is truly life. 1Timothy 6: 17-19

Incentives have always been part of the world of business. Without a motivational system, workers will likely be inclined to get by with minimum levels of effort and performance. The Bible recognizes the importance of motivation and rewards and has a surprising amount to say about this subject. Paul's words to the Corinthian church are a central passage in this regard:

"For we must all appear before the judgment seat of Christ, that each one may receive what is due him for the things done while in the body, whether good or bad" (2 Corinthians 5:10).

The Bible is filled with hundreds of practical truths, examples and principles about how we are to handle our money and our relationships. These scriptural laws and illustrations give us the keys to pleasing God, reflecting His giving nature, and receiving His generous abundance into our lives. One of the most important keys in successful attitudes is giving. It is a fundamental law of our covenant with God. God declares in Malachi 3: 6-12

"Since, I, the Lord, do not go back on my promises, you, sons of Jacob, have not perished. From the days of your ancestors you have ignored my commandments and have not kept them! Return to me, and I will return to you," says the Lord who rules over all. "But you say, 'How should we return?' Can a person rob God? You indeed are robbing me, but you say, 'How are we robbing you?' In tithes and contributions! You are bound for judgment because you are robbing me – this whole nation is guilty.

Bring the entire tithe into the storehouse so that there may be food in my temple. Test me in this matter," says the Lord who rules over all, "to see if I will not open for you the windows of heaven and pour out for you a blessing until there is no room for it all. Then I will stop the plague from ruining your crops, and the vine will not lose its fruit before harvest," says the Lord who rules over all. "All nations will call you happy, for you indeed will live in a delightful land," says the Lord who rules over all. "

Here is a divine promise you can key into to facilitate a change of attitude for your success. Start living a generous life, that is a life-style of giving, then you will not only experience fulfillment but also joy and true happiness. The Kingdom's bountiful harvest of blessings awaits all who will live by its principles and rule.

The success you build will not be based on what you accumulate for yourself. Rather, you will be remembered for what you have given. Mankind seeks to obtain and increase its money, food, clothes, possessions, houses, lands and businesses by expending energy in getting more and more "things" in the kingdom of God.

The Lord doesn't have a problem with our obtaining material possessions; but He does tell us that the way to achieve them is not by getting but by giving. As Jesus Himself tells us in Matthew 6:31-33, when we focus on seeking the ways of God (being a giver), material possessions will be given to us. No need to go out and struggle to get them in our own power; God will do the getting as we do the giving...

Generosity opens the doors to great destiny. Your generous spirit can expose incredible opportunities you might have never known God was offering you, blessings beyond your greatest desires and imagination. How much you want to receive of God's abundant blessings is in direct proportion to how much you give back of the blessings He has bestowed upon you.

The more you give, the more you will receive. Likewise, the more you receive, the more you should desire to give. Luke 6:38 tells us: "give and it shall be given unto you; good measure, pressed down, and shaken together, and running over, shall men give into your bosom. For with the same measure that ye mete withal it shall be measured to you again."

Take the example of a seed: When we plant an apple seed, we don't expect to harvest peaches. If we plant corn seeds, then corn is what we will harvest. It becomes important, then, to understand what we want to harvest. The kind of harvest you want determines the seed you need to sow. If you want more time, then you sow time to God, in serving Him. If you want more friendships, then you sow your friendship to others. If we want a harvest of money, then we need to sow money. Whatever we sow we will reap.

As believers, we seek to meet the needs we are presented with. If we have what people need, then that is what we are called to give. We are channels of provision from God to the people of this world. If God can get it through us, He will get it to us.

Once in God's Kingdom your mentality adjusts too - from deficit, debt, and scarcity - to abundance, satisfaction, and significance. YOU ARE A CHILD OF GOD! This demands continual adjustment in your thinking process (attitude).

Once in God's Kingdom, your desire to help others is revitalized. You know you should do it; and now you just do it! Of primary importance is persuading people to receive Jesus and develop their unique giftedness in serving other people. This takes much action and PATIENCE. Once in God's Kingdom, you learn how to live out the principles of God's Kingdom so you thrive in the world. This becomes your testimony of God's power, presence, and transformation. This advances God's Kingdom.

God wants you to be materially blessed. He has already made provision for this even before you were born. One reason many believers remain on the same spot is because they refuse to apply necessary principles of wealth creation.

We may teach others who apply it and receive the dividend, but as long as they do not apply it themselves, they remain located in poverty. The Lord will deliver you from poverty in Jesus' name, Amen!!

"Give and it shall be given unto you; good measure, pressed down, and shaken together, and running over, shall men give into your bosom. For with the same measure that ye mete withal it shall be measured to you again." (Luke 6:38)

This is a universal principle that applies both to believers and unbelievers. It does not say, 'Give and it shall be taken from you' but 'give and it shall be given unto you'. In other words, whenever you give, something is being handed over to you. This is so whether you believe it or not. Several people who were finding it difficult to make ends meet became born again, and as they applied this principle, they became millionaires.

Do you desire financial prosperity? How faithful are you to God's Kingdom in financial matters?

Chapter 9

The Power To Make Wealth

It is God who gave Israel the power to generate wealth. (Deuteronomy 8:18 NKJV)

"And you shall remember the LORD your God, for it is He who gives you power to get wealth." Wealth does not drop from the sky like manna. Wealth is created and generated by those who have understanding of their God-given power to 'get' wealth. Wealth must be created. Wisdom is the key, to make this happen. Praying for financial freedom is not enough to bring you to a lack-free zone. Practical wisdom skills are required for breakthrough in the area of finance. As we shall see later "the power to get wealth" is given by God in a specific way that is - the righteous person receives wisdom from God then diligently and ethically implements this wisdom and it is this diligent, wise and righteous implementation of wisdom and knowledge that generates this flow of prosperity.

Prosperity Flows To Those Who Fear God and Keep His Word. The relationship to God is primary as it is He who causes the blessings to flow and grants the power to make wealth. Shalom includes relational peace as well as financial prosperity for "he causes even their enemies to be at peace with them" (Proverbs 16:7).

The prosperity of those who live by the counsel of God and not of the world are stable and grows continually .The Bible says they shall prosper like a tree planted by the waters. And the labor of their hands prospers. (Psalm 1:1-3)

In Psalm 92:12-14 God's word further declares that those who are planted in God's house shall prosper even in old age.

Proverbs 10:22.God's plan for His children is blessings in abundance with no added sorrow. That's your portion in Jesus' name!

Prosperity Comes To Those Who Seek Wisdom and Understanding

Proverbs chapter 8 is the wisdom chapter of the Bible. In the right hand of wisdom is riches and honor.

Wisdom is insight and application of practical instruction base on Kingdom principles in the affairs of this life. Riches honor and long life becomes the natural outcome of walking in wisdom. To receive understanding and wisdom, you must seek for it as silver and gold. If you seek diligently and allow the Holy Spirit His freedom in your life, God will give you necessary keys and power to create a whole new world of abundance.

Prosperity Comes To Those Who Are Diligent

The best of instruction and wisdom will not walk without diligence and commitment. Plans are disappointed without dog-hearted commitment. Billion dollar ideas get rotten and become useless without 'diligent hands' being put to work Proverbs 21:5 says:

"The plans of the diligent surely lead to abundance, but everyone who is hasty only comes to want."

Diligence takes wisdom and carefully and energetically implements it to bring about prosperity. Diligence and God's blessing work together. Without diligence our blessings are not implemented and the people remain poor.

Psalm 1:3 says:

God will bless the labor of your hands. God does not pay premiums on laziness. Laziness and sluggishness will only rob you of your future and blessings. Get busy; seek God if you have been laid off your job. Pray about starting your own business. When one door seems to close...it's a signal that another is being opened. Look for the open doors around you.

Prosperity Is Retained By Righteous Living

(Proverbs 13:22-23 NKJV)
"A good man leaves an inheritance to his children's children, But the wealth of the sinner is stored up for the righteous."

Inter-generational wealth is God's plan for those who walk by His word. There is a transfer of wealth from the hands of the wicked to the righteous in these end time. The reason for this is the expansion of God's Kingdom. The gospel must be preached to all nations as a witness. To facilitate this end time evangelization, God is transferring the stored wealth of the wicked to the righteous.

Chapter 10

THEY ALL HAVE IT

There are countless examples of successful people abound in the Bible. Most probably, you have read these stories and treat them as children fables. We tend to lose sight of the fact that the men and women written about once lived right here on earth. Daniel, Deborah, Jehoshaphat, David, and Solomon, all of them were our predecessors in faith.

How do you demonstrate to God that you have the attitude for success? You can find out what pleases God through his Word. The Bible contains stories about real people like us. David is one of those biblical examples; let us observe how he became a man after God's own heart.

David was referred to as "a man after God's own heart" (Act 13:22) And when he had removed him, he raised up unto them David to be their king; to whom also he gave their testimony, and said, I have found David the son of Jesse, a man after mine own heart, which shall fulfill all my will.

He obviously possessed the attitude for success. God sought him out and made him King when he was the youngest of all the candidates in the house of Jesse. (1 Samuel 16: 1-12)

David was an ordinary youth, with many older brothers who were more spectacular, more brilliant and stronger. While everyone had a real job, he was assigned to the menial task of tending sheep. But he became God's anointed one. How? David demonstrated his attitude for success even while tending sheep

He was never afraid of the predators of the wild, and took that same attitude to the battlefield against Goliath. When he became the court musician to King Saul and bore the brunt of his madness, he never let that affected his attitude. Even when Saul overtly tried to kill him, he simply avoided a clash. He had an opportunity to kill Saul but his attitude never wavered.

More is written about David than any other character in the Bible. David has 66 Chapters written about him. Comparatively, Abraham and Joseph appeared in 14 Chapters each and Jacob has 11 Chapters. His name is mentioned in the Bible over 1,100 times. This should give us some idea of the significance of this man called David. He obviously had something different about him. Unarguably the greatest poems ever written to God were the Psalms, in a nutshell, David had the attitude for success and that pleased God.

Joshua was obviously not the oldest or wisest among the Israelites when Moses Died. (Deuteronomy 31: 1-5)

[1]And Moses went and spake these words unto all Israel.

And he said unto them, I am an hundred and twenty years old this day; I can no more go out and come in: also the LORD hath said unto me, Thou shalt not go over this Jordan.

The LORD thy God, he will go over before thee, and he will destroy these nations from before thee, and thou shalt possess them: and Joshua, he shall go over before thee, as the LORD hath said.
And the LORD shall do unto them as he did to Sihon and to Og, kings of the Amorites, and unto the land of them, whom he destroyed.
And the LORD shall give them up before your face, that ye may do unto them according unto all the commandments which I have commanded you.

What were his qualifications? What did God see in him? The truth is if God gives you promises, no matter the giants you meet on the way, muster a little boldness and you will see God give you a miracle.

Joshua wanted to claim God's promise and he refused to shy away from the challenges, not like many of us. We expect everything for nothing. Joshua had demonstrated the attitude for success when he was sent out among the twelve spies. (Numbers 13:130)

He and Caleb refused to be cowed by the strength of the Canaanites. And Caleb stilled the people before Moses, and said, Let us go up at once, and possess it; for we are well able to overcome it.
But the men that went up with him said, we be not able to go up against the people; for they are stronger than we. (Numbers 13:29-30)

It was a time of uncertainty for Israel. Moses had just died and been buried on Mount Pisgah (Joshua 1:1-9). Joshua had just taken the reins of leadership in Israel. He was to lead the children of Israel through to the Promised Land. To whom was he going to turn? What would he tell the people? Where would he go first? There must have been a million questions going through his mind.

Then, God speaks directly to Joshua. He tells Joshua to go over the Jordan and claim the land that God had given to them. He tells Joshua to observe the law and keep it faithfully. He then tells him to be strong and of good courage, be not afraid, neither be dismayed, and the Lord thy God is with thee. In essence he gives Joshua the keys to success. Joshua demonstrated the Success Attitude when he was sent along with eleven others on a spying mission. God came through for Joshua because of his attitude.

The story of Solomon also commands our attention. He was chosen to become King of Israel at a very young age. If his selection defies human logic, his attitude was certainly uniquely impressive. When he encountered the Lord, he asked not for money or for great wealth. With the success attitude he possessed, he knew just the right question to ask. He asked for wisdom from the Lord. (1 Kings 1: 3-15)

[5]In Gibeon the LORD appeared to Solomon in a dream by night: and God said, Ask what I shall give thee.
[6]And Solomon said, Thou hast shewed unto thy servant David my father great mercy, according as he walked before thee in truth, and in righteousness, and in uprightness of heart with thee; and thou hast kept for him this great kindness, that thou hast given him a son to sit on his throne, as it is this day.

[7]And now, O LORD my God, thou hast made thy servant king instead of David my father: and I am but a little child: I know not how to go out or come in.

[8]And thy servant is in the midst of thy people which thou hast chosen, a great people, that cannot be numbered nor counted for multitude.

Give therefore thy servant an understanding heart to judge thy people, that I may discern between good and bad: for who is able to judge this thy so great a people? And the speech pleased the LORD, that Solomon had asked this thing.

Ask yourself, if you were in Solomon's shoes, would you have requested for something as intangible as that?

What would you ask for? Wealth would probably be one of the most popular requests. Some think more money would solve almost all their problems. Good health might also rate high, particularly among those who have lost it. Happiness would be the leading desire for others. One worldwide poll of young people revealed happiness as the number one goal in life.

God responded and answered Solomon's prayers "[11]And God said unto him, Because thou hast asked this thing, and hast not asked for thyself long life; neither hast asked riches for thyself, nor hast asked the life of thine enemies; but hast asked for thyself understanding to discern judgment;

[12]Behold, I have done according to thy words: lo, I have given thee a wise and an understanding heart; so that there was none like thee before thee, neither after thee shall any arise like unto thee.

[13]And I have also given thee that which thou hast not asked, both riches, and honour: so that there shall not be any among the kings like unto thee all thy days.

Scripture testifies that all Israel "saw that the wisdom of God was in him" (1 Kings 3:28)

Now I know you have a burning question, what exactly are the attitudes for success? You may have attended a lot of seminars where they profess to teach you successful attitude. But, from the Bible's viewpoint, attitude to success is more than all the laws propounded by the motivational speakers. Some of the Biblical laws are already obvious in the preceding paragraphs. But let's seek to clarify these principles.

One, the strength of your faith, as shown by the example of Solomon.

He could have asked for anything under the sun, but he chose to ask for wisdom for he had faith that God knows the depth of his heart. (Mathew 17:20) teaches us that "For truly I say to you, if you have faith as a mustard seed, you shall say to this mountain, "Move from here to there" and it shall move; and nothing shall be impossible to you."

Two, courage in the face of adversity.

Joshua had this and refused to be weighed down by the perceived might of his adversaries. "The Lord is my light and my salvation; whom shall I fear? The Lord is the strength of my life; of whom shall I be afraid? Psalm 27:1" God has always been attentive to the courageous, the book of Deuteronomy 31:8 says "The Lord himself goes before you and will be with you; he will never leave you nor forsake you. Do not be afraid; do not be discouraged.

Third, David's attitude and motive

He always sought to please God in his actions. he prayed, sang and fought, all for the glory of God! Obedience remains a vital attitude to success, for God to look your way; you have to follow his words, practice his principles and do all that he commands. In John 14:23, Jesus spoke "If anyone loves me, he will obey my teaching. My Father will love him, and we will come to him and make our home with him. You also cannot afford to be lazy. Don't expect God to give you a miracle and also help you claim it physically. Some of you have turned the Lord into an errand boy. You think that because you are a son of God that you do not have any need to work hard. Another obvious success attitude exemplified by David was his habitual life of praise, worship and thanksgiving. If you cannot thank God enough for what he has given you, you may not be a candidate for another. Many of us take our blessings for granted. Start to thank Him for every thing he has done and He will surprise you by doing more and more.

Chapter 11

YOU HAVE TO WANT IT

In Matthew 11:11,12 The Lord tells us: Verily I say unto you, among them that are born of women there hath not risen a greater than John the Baptist: notwithstanding he that is least in the kingdom of heaven is greater than he.
And from the days of John the Baptist until now the kingdom of heaven suffereth violence and the violent take it by force.

Walking in kingdom success demands more than a mere prayer request. There is absolutely no way that you can divorce what you want and passionately seek from what you will get. The Scriptures teach that it is not mercenary to be motivated by reward; instead, Jesus encouraged us to long to hear the words,

"Well done, good and faithful servant! You have been faithful with a few things; I will put you in charge of many things. Come and share your master's happiness" (Matthew 25:21, 23).

The New Testament is replete with invitations to pursue God's rewards, affirming that they will prove to be more than worth the cost.

"Blessed is the man who perseveres under trial, because when he has stood the test, he will receive the crown of life that God has promised to those who love him" (James 1:12).

God has plans for us in spite of our present circumstances. We work in an imperfect workplace, thus our work is imperfect. No matter how ideally suited for your present job you may be, you know that pain of unrealized potential, lost opportunity and the frustration borne of a lack of recognition. Even in the best work environments, there exists something of politics, laziness or gossip.

God longs to bless and reward his people, but it is essential that they be willing to turn to him and repent of their unfaithfulness and disobedience.

"You will seek me and find me when you seek me with all your heart" (v. 13). We serve a God who "rewards those who earnestly seek him" (Hebrews 11:6). God actually enjoys bestowing benefits on those who turn to him in dependence and trust, and he hates the judgment that sin and rebellion entail. Your zeal, drive and demand from God for financial excellence, prosperity and success will determine how much you get from Him. Nobody will give you something you obviously don't want. You have to convince God that you really want it.

In Deuteronomy 30:19 God spoke to us thus: "This day I call heaven and earth as witnesses against you that I have set before you life and death, blessings and curses. Now choose life, so that you and your children may live".

If God consistently reveals such a passion for our highest good, why do we so often struggle with seeking him and the rewards he offers? If the Scriptures have so much to say about rewards, why is so little attention given to this topic?

In (Nehemiah 1:11) we read Nehemiah's prayer for success; Please, O Lord, listen attentively to the prayer of your servant and to the prayer of your servants who take pleasure in showing respect to your name. Grant your servant success today and show compassion to me in the presence of this man."

That was a man asking for something he wanted. His words and desire couldn't have been clearer. When you show God how much you desire something, and also how helpless you are in your own strength, you are giving Him the perfect setting for a miracle.

"Ask, and it shall be given you; seek, and ye shall find; knock, and it shall be opened unto you: for every one that asketh receiveth; and he that seeketh findeth; and to him that knocketh it shall be opened." (Matthew 7:7-8)

Chapter 12

I WILL NOT BE DENIED

Our God is an all-powerful, holy, holy, holy God. It is not unusual for someone who encounters God in his holy splendor to prostrate himself flat on his or her face in fearful reference. The call of Isaiah in Isaiah 6 is a classic example of this. The covenant people of God at the base of Mount Sinai had a similar reaction. The holy presence of God covered the top of Mount Sinai with smoke, thunder and lightning along with his great voice. They were so fearful that they wanted to hear the voice of the Lord no more, and asked Moses to be their mediator so they would not have to hear God's voice directly.

Knowing this about our God, only few believers would dare plead their case. Let's look at some examples of those who boldly pleaded their case with the Almighty and refused to be denied of their request.

The first example comes from Genesis 18:22-33. God reveals to Abraham that he will destroy Sodom and Gomorrah because of their wickedness. And the LORD said, Because the cry of Sodom and Gomorrah is great, and because their sin is very grievous; I will go down now, and see whether they have done altogether according to the cry of it, which is come unto me; and if not, I will know. And the men turned their faces from thence, and went toward Sodom, but Abraham stood yet before the LORD.

And Abraham drew near, and said, Wilt thou also destroy the righteous with the wicked? Peradventure there be fifty righteous within the city: wilt thou also destroy and not spare the place for the fifty righteous that are therein? That be far from thee to do after this manner, to slay the righteous with the wicked: and that the righteous should be as the wicked, that be far from thee: Shall not the Judge of all the earth do right?

And the LORD said, If I find in Sodom fifty righteous within the city, then I will spare all the place for their sakes. And Abraham answered and said, Behold now, I have taken upon me to speak unto the LORD, which am but dust and ashes: Peradventure there shall lack five of the fifty righteous: wilt thou destroy all the city for lack of five? And he said, If I find there forty and five, I will not destroy it. And he spake unto him yet again, and said, Peradventure there shall be forty found there. And he said, I will not do it for forty's sake. And he said unto him, Oh let not the LORD be angry, and I will speak: Peradventure there shall thirty be found there. And he said, I will not do it, if I find thirty there. And he said, Behold now, I have taken upon me to speak unto the LORD: Peradventure there shall be twenty found there. And he said I will not destroy it for twenty's sake.

And he said Oh let not the LORD be angry, and I will speak yet but this once: Peradventure ten shall be found there. And he said I will not destroy it for ten's sake.

Verse 20. Shows the awfulness of wickedness and sin. Cities that are so wicked would have a reputation for being so. Like Corinth which had a reputation for all vices of immorality God had every right to destroy these cities, and it is likely that anyone who knew anything about these cities would agree.

Then Abraham does the unthinkable. No, it isn't that Abraham tries to change God's mind. It isn't even that he tries to bargain with God to spare the city for a handful of righteous people if they are found in the city. It is in his bold question which could implicate God - "Far be it from you to do such a thing, to slay the righteous with the wicked, so that the righteous and the wicked are treated alike. Far be it from you! Shall not the judge of all the earth deal justly?" Wait a minute! What is Abraham saying? Is he speaking foolishly and ignorantly? Why would Abraham say such a thing? Does Abraham believe God would do a grave injustice by slaying the innocent along with the wicked?

Abraham knows he is going out on a limb, so he pleads with God not to get angry as he tries to save the city, a wicked city at that. If there was any doubt about the justice of the destruction of Sodom and Gomorrah, the encounter between Abraham and God and subsequent salvation of Lot and his family has removed all doubt as to God's justice in destroying every man and woman in the city. As can be clearly seen, Abraham rejected denial of what he wanted. He interceded and pleaded with God for mercy.

He could have stood by meekly and watch as the destruction took place, but he placed himself right in God's path and made this powerful plea for God to change His decision to destroy Sodom and Gomorrah. God saw it in Abraham tenacity and mindset that refuses to be denied. He walked with God in this high level of intimacy so much so that God said in vs 12,13: And the LORD said, Shall I hide from Abraham that thing which I do;

Seeing that Abraham shall surely become a great and mighty nation and all the nations of the earth shall be blessed in him?

This beautiful fellowship and intimacy with God allowed Abraham to boldly state his case, interceded and pleaded his case with God.

Our next example is Moses. God made a covenant with the newly formed nation of Israel at Mount Sinai in Exodus 19..In vs 8 Israel promised to loyalty and obedience to God and His word. They said "All that the Lord has spoken we will do"...

Just over a month later, they built an idol and had a feast to the Lord. In response, God tells Moses to "let me alone, that my anger may burn against them and that I may destroy them; and I will make of you a great nation." (Ex 32:10).

There was no doubt that the people were guilty. God redeemed them out of Egyptian bondage to be his own people, and now they are already rebelling. There was no doubt that God would be justified when He carries out his intent to destroy these people.

"Let me alone so that ...?"

Could Moses had actually stop God from unleashing his wrath?

In saying this, God practically invites Moses to intervene. Just as God revealed to Abraham what he was going to do to Sodom and Gomorrah, thereby allowing Abraham to respond, God appears to do the same with Moses. So Moses responds.

Moses cannot appeal to justice because it is clear that God is justified in destroying these people. Moses appeals to God's promise to the Patriarchs recorded in Genesis. But this appeal does not carry much weight because God could destroy the people in the wilderness, start over with Moses, and still be faithful to his promise.

So what can Moses do? What can he say? Then Moses entreated the Lord his God, and said 'O Lord, why does your anger burn against your people whom you have brought out from the land of Egypt with great power and with a mighty hand?' " (Ex 32:10). God called them "this" people, but Moses continues to call them "your" people. It is interesting that Moses' words sound very much like some of the Psalms. Moses uses the language of prayer when he addresses God. In the end, Moses convinces God to "change his mind" concerning the destruction of Israel. Moses' ability to present and plead his case as Israel's "intercessor" saved the nation..

Another example comes from Amos 7:1-7. Twice God announces judgment on Israel in two visions. Twice, Amos pleads with God, and twice God relents. The picture the author paints of the nation and her sins in the previous six chapters of Amos makes it clear that God is justified in unleashing his wrath against Israel. God had caused the nation to become prosperous. However, many were getting rich at the expense of the poor, so God decides to withdraw his blessing and unleash his judgment. He reveals to Amos through visions what he intends to do, yet Amos manages to swerve the nature of God's judgment.

However, there is something unique about the examples above. What is amazing is that God intentionally involves men in his decisions. Moses could have consented and said, "I'm just your slave, I can't stop you. Besides, you're the boss, do what you see is best".

Instead, Moses, understanding the power of his ability to intercede, pleads his case and has the honor of God giving attention to his plea.

In Exodus 6. He reveals his personal name! One does not go around offering his name to others for no reason. When you introduce your name, you are initiating some sort of relationship. When you initiate a relationship with another, you become "vulnerable" to that other person's needs, wants, and wishes. You also increase the potential of being hurt by that other person as well. So being able to know and use another's name is both a privilege and a responsibility. We usually don't think of God in these terms, but here you have it, preserved for us in scripture to teach us the possibility a man can go with God.

So the book of Exodus is about how God initiates a relationship with the people of Israel. The Book of Exodus begins with the absence of God, and ends with God filling the tabernacle and living among his people. Since God desires a relationship with his people, he at times invites his people to be a part of his decisions. Isn't that amazing?

Hezekiah was supposed to die, but he pleaded with God to let him live a little longer. God granted him his request.

(2 Kings 20: 1-11) Is your faith strong enough to plead your case through? Can you build the courage against denial?

The mind-set of "I will not be denied" of that which I know is scriptural and rightfully mine is a key to a life of success and abundant prosperity.

Chapter 13

HUMILITY WITH DIGNITY

It will be inconceivable for a child to order his father around. As Apostle Peter wrote in (1 Peter 5:6) "Humble yourselves therefore under the mighty hand of God, that he may exalt you in due time."

The scriptures command us to humble ourselves. What is humility? Humility is accepting our selves as we really are before God. It is like standing on a cliff looking across the valley far below and hearing God tell us to keep going. The valley was made for us to cross it, but it is such a long way down! Most people decide not to cross. They, like Nebuchadnezzar, refuse to listen to God's warning and choose to persist in their pride instead. For Nebuchadnezzar, it was only twelve months later when God confronted him and tossed him from earth's highest cliff to its lowest abyss. For seven years, he went across the fields as a beast (Daniel 4).

God had warned each one of them to humble themselves. But each one of them stubbornly resisted taking the steps down to humility. They thought far too much of their position in life, their self-gratification of desires and confidence in their wealth. They only needed time before they fell over the cliff. That is a hard way to meet humility.

Humility, though neglected, stands as one of the foundational teachings for having a growing and fruitful Christian life. In a real sense humility holds the secret for growth, wisdom, perseverance, blessing, salvation, and wonderful relationships. I am literally humbled by the way I have lived so long as a Christian and heard so little emphasis placed on the importance humility plays in our Christian lives. Jesus placed great emphasis on humility.

"Whoever then humbles himself as this child, he is the greatest in the Kingdom of heaven." (Matthew 18:4). We do not naturally seek the path of humility. But if we seek to be successful or great, then we must learn to humble ourselves.

God does not take a man to great heights without first walking him through the darkness of the valley. Our pathway has been beautifully carved out by the glorious and gracious Lord Jesus Christ.

We have encouraged many people to grow in Christ but rarely, if at all, have we ever heard anyone teach that we should pursue humility. For the first time, Jesus again spoke of entering the Kingdom in Matthew 5:3, "Blessed are the poor in spirit, for theirs is the Kingdom of heaven."

Circumstances in life are designed to humble us, not crush us. They are experiences that shape us so that we may taste and have life to the fullest. We look at such experiences as threats to our success, but they are the path to true success. If you follow the path. God illustrates this truth in nature all around us. We are literally surrounded by the 'humbling' principle but the world knows nothing of it.

Just think how the leaves must drop and strip the trees of their glory. Seeds need to descend from their lofty and glorious setting only to be miserably buried in the mud. It is only then, does new life become evident. We have a winter of souls too. God's humbling of our soul is part of His good plan for our lives, not some extraneous interruption that must be avoided at all costs.

Jesus said, "My will is to do the will of my Father." May this also be our hearts' prayer. The only thing that should consume us is the accomplishment of our Father's will. Like Moses, we face two main problems getting God's work done. Both of these problems originate in pride. In fact, we are really self-focused.

1) Self-confidence. We believe we can do all sorts of things for God. This often manifests itself in our youth when we are confident, energetic, healthy and full of hope.

2) Self-pity. We are convinced we are so valuable to God but are disgruntled over not having the opportunity to do more. This often occurs when we are older and experienced. Our health begins to fail. We feel 'cheated' out of life's opportunities. We believe our complaining and moaning are proper because our situation limits us from doing what we want.

His first forty years were in the palace where he gained his self-confidence; his second forty years took place in the wilderness where he exhibited self-pity. These first eighty years were like spiritual boot camp where his self-confidence

73

and self-pity were emptied out so that finally God could do His work in and through Moses' life.

Moses, I believe, experienced the same pride problems that we face, and yet God managed to do His mighty works through his life. Moses was self-confident. Raised in the greatest palace in the world at that time, he received all the top education and authority.

We remember how Moses killed a Hebrew oppressor. He fled Egypt. God used that training in Moses' life but not in the way he thought. Moses fled into the wilderness for his second forty years of life. Now he was hopeless. He couldn't do anything for God there. Used to a metropolitan area, power, and control, now he had to face a handful of people and shepherd sheep.

PREPARATION WITH OPPORTUNITY

Most of us know the disappointment of lost opportunities. Someone calls and invites us to attend a concert with them. We feel a bit lazy and say, "No, I'll stay home tonight." The next day we hear that the concert was totally awesome. We think wow, I missed something good.

Some of us kick ourselves for not investing more money in real estate fifteen years ago. We missed a wave of increasing values. A lament I hear frequently from parents is, "I missed the boat with my children and didn't spend the time with them that I should have spent. We also remember times we were extra sensitive to the Spirit of God. We rejected the good choices He was urging us to make. We missed the wave of God's blessing and suffered much heartache.

On the other hand we have experienced the joy and exhilaration of making good choices and decisions. Perhaps we were given Biblical advice about dating, relationships and character. Seventy years later we're still riding this incredible wave of God's blessing.

Jesus saw that the people of His day were in great danger of missing God's wave of blessing. For hundreds of years they waited for the coming of their Messiah. When He came in the person of Jesus, many of them rejected Him.

Three days before His crucifixion Jesus told the parable of the Ten Virgins to illustrate how they were missing the Messiah's blessing. To better understand this parable you must know the three stages to Eastern marriages in Jesus' culture.

First came the engagement in which a formal settlement was made by the fathers of the bride and groom. Second a betrothal ceremony was held at the home of the bride's parent's where mutual promises were exchanged and the groom gave the bride presents. The betrothal was almost as strong as the marriage. Third, the marriage occurred about one year after betrothal. The groom brought his bride to his house for the marriage feast. She was accompanied from her father's house by her bridesmaids. The procession meets the virgins of the parable at a convenient place and leads them to the banquet hall.

Here is the parable as told by Jesus. "The Kingdom of Heaven can be illustrated by the story of ten bridesmaids who took their lamps and went to meet the bridegroom. But only five of them were wise enough to fill their lamps with oil, while the other five were foolish and forgot.

"So, when the bridegroom was delayed, they lay down to rest until midnight, when they were roused by the shout, 'The bridegroom is coming! Come out and welcome him!' "All the girls jumped up and trimmed their lamps. Then the five who hadn't any oil begged the others to share with them, for their lamps were going out. "But the others replied, 'We haven't enough. Go instead to the shops and buy some for yourselves.' "But while they were gone, the bridegroom came, and those who were ready went in with him to the marriage feast, and the door was locked.

"Later, when the other five returned, they stood outside, calling, 'Sir, open the door for us!' "But he called back, 'Go away! It is too late!' "So stay awake and be prepared, for you do not know the date or moment of my return. (Matthew 25:1-13 TLB)

Many people miss the timeless application of this parable by thinking it only applies to what we call "The Second Coming of Christ." That's the event that Peter was referring to when he wrote, "But the day of the Lord will come like a thief. The heavens will disappear with a roar; the elements will be destroyed by fire, and the earth and everything in it will be laid bare. . . But in keeping with his promise we are looking forward to a new heaven and a new earth, the home of righteousness." (2 Peter 3:9-13 NIV)

Please do not fall into the trap of limiting the application of this parable to being ready for the second coming of Christ. The parable's last verse says, "Watch therefore, for you know neither the day nor the hour in which the Son of Man is coming." (Matthew 25:13)

The key to understanding this parable is the words, "the Son of Man is coming." The truth of scripture is that at unexpected times Christ comes to all of us, either in blessing or condemnation. That's why we are exhorted to be waiting and watchful.

In Jesus' day many people were not prepared in heart, mind and soul for the Messiah's coming to them. They would not repent of their ungodly actions and attitudes. These people were religious but not godly. Religious people go through the forms of worship to keep alive the nostalgia of their past. For them, worship was only an intellectual exercise that left out the heart. Godly people worship with their heart and head. Godly people live to glorify God and to enjoy Him forever. Religious people live for the success of the organization. Godly people are looking for the wave of God's blessing. Religious people try to make their own waves of blessing.

Church history tells of many times when Christ came to a community or a nation in revival blessing. These were times when the holiness of God burned like a refiner's fire. Before the service would begin people would come streaming to the altar to get right with God. Church services were not advertised and yet the unchurched felt an unexplainable compulsion to come into a church building and kneel in repentance before God. At some places people would fall on their faces in the streets and cry out to God for mercy. These events were giant waves of God's blessing, the coming of the Lord to these people.

There is also the sense in which Christ comes to us daily in little things. It may be in the hand of friendship that someone offers to us. We reach out and grasp that hand of friendship and it grows into a relationship that blesses us for the rest of our lives.

The coming of the Lord to us may be a word of caution. "Don't marry that person," is His warning. Some people reject God's caution and a life of heartache follows. Others catch the wave of God's blessing and sixty years later they are still on their spiritual surf boards having the ride of their lives. The Lord may come to us with this word of opportunity, "Study hard, specialize in this area of knowledge and the wave of my blessing will make you a blessing to the peoples of the earth."

The salvation of the Lord is a very broad term that encompasses all time and the entire person; body, soul and spirit. For too many years we have limited its application to the eternal salvation of our soul.

The salvation that Jesus bought for us on the cross gives us quality living today and the security of our soul in Heaven tomorrow. Question! What great blessings are you missing today because your religious eyes do not see the wave of blessing God is offering you today?

Jesus told parables to make a point that people would never forget. What was it about this story that would have stuck in their hearts forever? What was the emotional hook? The first event that grabbed Jesus' audience was the fact that five virgins were dressed for the event but failed to make the necessary preparations to fulfill their roles in the ceremony. The main thing is to focus on the main thing. If you do that, you'll always catch the wave of God's blessing.

The second event that grabbed Jesus' audience was the emotional heartbreak of being locked out of the wedding celebration. The five wise virgins could not rescue them from their irresponsibility. Jerusalem had no Lube oil stores. There is a certain finality to the words, "and the door was locked."

78

I've read of young people who cried on their wedding night. Why? Because on one night of careless passion, they gave away their virginity. Once that is lost its like "and the door is locked."

I know many parents who neglected their children in the formative years of their lives. They miss the golden opportunity of a little child's innocence. One day they discover that the door is locked, to their child's heart. Some children are so bitter that they never open the door. Other people get in with the wrong crowd. One thing leads to another and eventually they have a prison record. Too late they discover that a prison record locks some key doors to their future and they miss the wave of God's blessing in their lives.

That Biblical phrase "and the door was locked," talks about missed opportunities that are gone forever and ever and ever and ever. No matter how long you cry, "God give me back my virginity, God give me a second chance with my children, God let me try that business deal one more time, or God give me another chance so that jail record can be wiped from my slate." God says, "Sorry, the clock cannot be rolled back, the door to yesterday is locked forever, you missed that wave of blessing."

You may say, "But God, just this once roll back the clock, I didn't mean what I did." From Heaven we hear the words, "I'm sorry but my word says, and the door was locked." This phrase also talks about the opportunity for an eternal home in Heaven. It talks about a day when there will be no second chances. The massive doors of time will close and forever will begin. You will either be at the Lord's banquet table in paradise or you will find yourself where the worm does not die and the fire is not quenched.

Even if you were to wail with honest, heart felt integrity, "Lord! Lord! Open the door for me!" He will reply with words that will melt your bones, "I tell you the truth, I don't know you." The wave of eternal blessing will have passed over you. Thus, the main point of the parable is, "Therefore keep watch, because you do not know the day or the hour when the final wave of God's blessing rolls past you." Have you trusted yourself fully to Jesus?

Have you ever invited Jesus into your life in words that expressed the following thoughts? "Lord Jesus, I want to know you personally. Thank You for dying on the cross for my sins. I open the door of my life and receive you as my Savior and Lord. Thank You for forgiving my sins and giving me eternal life. Take control of the throne of my life. Make me the kind of person you want me to be.

Be diligent in serving the Lord be diligent in maintaining your relationship with Jesus. Be diligent in prayer. If you do these things you'll find yourself riding through life on the crest of the mother of all waves. Don't miss the wave of God's blessing.